FRENCH
WORD GAMES
AND
PUZZLES

Sister Chantal

DOVER PUBLICATIONS, INC.
New York

INTRODUCTION

This book contains a variety of entertaining puzzles designed to assist in building basic French vocabulary. There are four different types of activity, and each puzzle's words are unified by a specific theme.

Solutions appear beginning on page 47, and an Alphabetical Word List of all French words used in the book (with indications of the gender of nouns) begins on page 57.

Bibliographical Note

French Word Games and Puzzles is a new work, first published by Dover Publications, Inc., in 1995.

International Standard Book Number: 0-486-28481-6

Manufactured in the United States of America
Dover Publications, Inc., 31 East 2nd Street, Mineola, N.Y. 11501

SEARCH-A-WORDS

1. **La Famille** / The Family

Find 16 words for different members of a family that are hidden in this letter grid. The words may appear vertically, horizontally or diagonally and may overlap or be reversed. Find and circle the hidden words, then write them in the spaces at the bottom of the page (accents, hyphens and ligatures are omitted from the grids). Each word's first letter and English equivalent are provided as clues.

G	F	E	N	F	A	N	T	G
C	R	P	M	S	O	E	U	R
E	E	A	O	B	E	N	E	A
N	R	R	N	U	R	I	V	N
I	E	E	C	D	E	E	E	D
S	B	N	L	A	P	C	N	M
U	E	T	E	P	M	E	R	E
O	B	T	A	N	T	E	R	R
C	O	U	S	I	N	E	E	

b_____ (baby)   m_____ (mother)

c_____ (cousin [M])   n_____ (nephew)

c_____ (cousin [F])   n_____ (niece)

e_____ (child)   o_____ (uncle)

f_____ (brother)   p_____ (relative)

g_____ (grandmother)   p_____ (father)

g_____ (grandfather)   s_____ (sister)

m_____ (husband)   t_____ (aunt)

2. Le Corps / The Body

Find eleven words for parts of the body. The words may appear vertically, horizontally or diagonally and may overlap or be reversed. Find and circle the hidden words, then write them in the spaces at the bottom of the page (accents, hyphens and ligatures are omitted from the grids). Each word's first letter and English equivalent are provided as clues.

C	H	E	V	E	U	X
O	S	R	D	E	I	P
U	A	T	M	A	I	N
O	R	E	I	L	L	E
E	B	T	B	D	U	N
I	N	E	Z	O	M	V
L	C	O	J	S	Q	F

b_____ (arm)

c_____ (hair)

c_____ (neck)

d_____ (back)

j_____ (cheek)

m_____ (hand)

n_____ (nose)

o_____ (eye)

o_____ (ear)

p_____ (foot)

t_____ (head)

3. Les Adjectifs I / Adjectives I

Find 12 common adjectives (all are given in masculine singular form). The words may appear vertically, horizontally or diagonally and may overlap or be reversed. Find and circle the hidden words, then write them in the spaces at the bottom of the page (accents, hyphens and ligatures are omitted from the grids). Each word's first letter and English equivalent are provided as clues.

N	C	H	A	U	D	V
L	O	N	G	R	E	I
A	U	U	O	U	R	E
R	R	I	V	D	M	U
G	T	I	T	E	P	X
E	L	A	I	D	A	A
R	P	C	B	E	A	U

b_____ (beautiful)

c_____ (warm; hot)

c_____ (short)

d_____ (straight)

d_____ (hard)

l_____ (ugly)

l_____ (wide; broad)

l_____ (long)

n_____ (new)

p_____ (small; young)

r_____ (rough)

v_____ (old)

4. La Maison / The House

Find nine words associated with houses. The words may appear vertically, horizontally or diagonally and may overlap or be reversed. Find and circle the hidden words, then write them in the spaces at the bottom of the page (accents, hyphens and ligatures are omitted from the grids). Each word's first letter and English equivalent are provided as clues.

C	T	O	I	T	R	F
U	H	S	B	M	E	E
I	P	A	K	E	I	N
S	O	L	M	U	N	E
I	R	O	U	B	E	T
N	T	N	R	L	R	R
E	E	K	B	E	G	E

c_____ ([bed]room)

c_____ (kitchen)

f_____ (window)

g_____ (attic, loft)

m_____ (piece of furniture)

m_____ (wall)

p_____ (door)

s_____ (living room)

t_____ (roof)

5. Le Temps / Weather

Find nine weather-related nouns. The words may appear vertically, horizontally or diagonally and may overlap or be reversed. Find and circle the hidden words, then write them in the spaces at the bottom of the page (accents, hyphens and ligatures are omitted from the grids). Each word's first letter and English equivalent are provided as clues.

V	B	E	I	U	L	P	G
F	E	C	H	I	K	J	L
R	D	N	E	I	G	E	A
A	C	L	T	B	G	D	C
I	O	D	I	O	R	F	E
S	C	H	A	U	D	H	I

c_____ (hot)   n_____ (snow)

f_____ (cool)   p_____ (rain)

f_____ (cold)   s_____ (sun)

g_____ (frost)   v_____ (wind)

g_____ (ice)

6. Les Animaux de Basse-cour / Farm Animals

Find the names of 13 farm animals. The words may appear vertically, horizontally or diagonally and may overlap or be reversed. Find and circle the hidden words, then write them in the spaces at the bottom of the page (accents, hyphens and ligatures are omitted from the grids). Each word's first letter and English equivalent are provided as clues.

P	M	D	R	A	N	A	C
O	O	Y	O	N	L	H	N
U	U	U	V	E	A	U	N
S	T	B	L	T	V	Q	I
S	O	I	E	E	E	O	P
I	N	N	E	I	H	C	A
N	O	H	C	O	C	C	L

a_____ (donkey)   l _____ (rabbit)

c_____ (duck)   m_____ (sheep)

c_____ (cat [M])   o_____ (goose)

c_____ (horse)   p_____ (hen)

c_____ (dog [M])   p_____ (chick)

c_____ (pig)   v_____ (calf)

c_____ (rooster)

7. Le Transport / Transportation

Find the words for nine forms of transportation (many are short, colloquial forms). The words may appear vertically, horizontally or diagonally and may overlap or be reversed. Find and circle the hidden words, then write them in the spaces at the bottom of the page (accents, hyphens and ligatures are omitted from the grids). Each word's first letter and English equivalent are provided as clues.

A	D	B	I	X	A	T
N	U	A	V	I	O	N
O	O	T	R	A	I	N
I	R	E	O	T	U	L
M	T	A	T	B	M	U
A	E	U	O	T	U	A
C	M	U	M	I	V	S

a_____ (car)

a_____ (bus)

a_____ (airplane)

b_____ (boat)

c_____ (truck)

m_____ (subway)

m_____ (motorcycle)

t_____ (taxicab)

t_____ (train)

8. Au Téléphone / On the Telephone

Find the infinitive forms of nine telephone-related verbs. The words may appear vertically, horizontally or diagonally and may overlap or be reversed. Find and circle the hidden words, then write them in the spaces at the bottom of the page (accents, hyphens and ligatures are omitted from the grids). Each word's first letter and English equivalent are provided as clues.

M	A	S	P	A	R	L	E	R	A
T	E	L	E	P	H	O	N	E	R
M	C	O	M	P	O	S	E	R	S
A	E	M	R	E	T	U	O	C	E
S	R	R	E	L	E	P	P	A	R
A	I	M	R	E	N	N	O	S	M
S	D	E	C	R	O	C	H	E	R

a_____ (to call) p_____ (to talk)

c_____ (to dial) r_____ (to call back)

d_____ (to pick up s_____ (to ring)
[the receiver])

d_____ (to say) t_____ (to phone)

e_____ (to listen)

9. Les Salutations / Greetings

Find eight words relating to conversations or greetings. The words may appear vertically, horizontally or diagonally and may overlap or be reversed. Find and circle the hidden words, then write them in the spaces at the bottom of the page (accents, hyphens and ligatures are omitted from the grids). Each word's first letter and English equivalent are provided as clues.

B	O	N	S	O	I	R	C	S
O	I	S	A	L	U	E	R	O
N	L	E	R	E	C	I	R	U
J	E	L	N	R	O	C	R	H
O	C	R	A	V	E	E	C	A
U	E	C	E	C	E	R	E	I
R	R	R	C	R	E	N	C	T
T	U	L	A	S	R	C	U	E
A	C	R	E	C	R	E	T	R

a_____ (hello [on phone])   b_____ (good evening)

a_____ (so long)   s_____ (to greet)

b_____ (welcome)   s_____ (hi)

b_____ (good morning)   s_____ (to wish)

10. Le Voyage / Travel

Find 19 travel-related words. The words may appear vertically, horizontally or diagonally and may overlap or be reversed. Find and circle the hidden words, then write them in the spaces at the bottom of the page (accents, hyphens and ligatures are omitted from the grids). Each word's first letter and English equivalent are provided as clues.

V	K	L	S	E	D	I	U	G	P	S
A	I	I	M	S	N	O	I	V	A	O
C	M	S	B	I	L	L	E	T	S	P
A	E	G	A	L	P	E	T	I	S	E
N	O	I	T	A	V	R	E	S	E	R
C	R	I	O	V	O	T	O	H	P	K
E	C	A	R	T	E	N	A	U	O	D
S	E	G	A	G	A	B	L	M	R	B
H	O	T	E	L	N	I	A	R	T	A

a_____ (friends [M])   p_____ (beach)

a_____ (airplane)   r_____ (rest)

b_____ (luggage)   r_____ (reservation)

b_____ (ticket)   s_____ (point of interest)

c_____ (map)   t_____ (train)

d_____ (customs)   v_____ (vacation)

g_____ (guide)   v_____ (suitcase)

h_____ (hotel)   v_____ (visa)

p_____ (passport)   v_____ (to see)

p_____ (photograph)

11. Au Bord de la Mer / At the Beach

Find eleven words relating to the beach. The words may appear vertically, horizontally or diagonally and may overlap or be reversed. Find and circle the hidden words, then write them in the spaces at the bottom of the page (accents, hyphens and ligatures are omitted from the grids). Each word's first letter and English equivalent are provided as clues.

N	C	H	R	I	V	A	G	E
O	E	E	E	A	V	M	L	B
S	N	A	G	E	R	E	I	R
S	A	U	N	A	A	R	E	O
I	E	B	O	L	L	O	L	N
O	U	R	L	S	E	P	O	Z
P	P	R	P	E	S	I	S	E

b_____ (tanned)   r_____ (shore)

m_____ (sea)   s_____ (sand)

n_____ (to swim)   s_____ (salt)

p_____ (beach)   s_____ (sun)

p_____ (to dive)   v_____ (wave)

p_____ (fish)

12. Les Pays / Countries

Find the names of 14 countries. The words may appear vertically, horizontally or diagonally and may overlap or be reversed. Find and circle the hidden words, then write them in the spaces at the bottom of the page (accents, hyphens and ligatures are omitted from the grids). Each word's first letter and English equivalent are provided as clues.

G	B	S	A	C	A	N	A	D	A
E	R	U	N	H	A	N	E	N	L
S	U	E	P	I	O	I	G	E	L
P	S	D	C	N	R	L	S	E	E
A	S	E	O	E	E	S	J	E	M
G	I	R	A	T	I	A	N	I	A
N	E	G	E	U	P	E	N	L	G
E	P	R	S	O	R	D	U	A	N
F	R	A	N	C	E	N	E	T	E
E	I	R	G	N	O	H	E	I	T

A_____ (Germany)   H_____ (Hungary)

A_____ (England)   I_____ (India)

C_____ (Canada)   I_____ (Italy)

C_____ (China)   J_____ (Japan)

E_____ (Spain)   R_____ (Russia)

F_____ (France)   S_____ (Sweden)

G_____ (Greece)   S_____ (Switzerland)

13. Les Jours de la Semaine / The Days of the Week

Find the names of the seven days of the week. The words may appear vertically, horizontally or diagonally and may overlap or be reversed. Find and circle the hidden words, then write them in the spaces at the bottom of the page (accents, hyphens and ligatures are omitted from the grids). Each word's first letter and English equivalent are provided as clues.

M	V	C	J	E	U	D	I	E
E	R	E	A	V	A	T	H	T
R	E	L	N	O	M	C	E	L
C	E	U	T	D	N	T	E	O
R	E	N	M	A	R	D	I	U
E	F	D	M	P	E	E	L	L
D	E	I	S	A	M	E	D	I
I	D	N	E	I	G	E	O	I

D_____ (Sunday)   J_____ (Thursday)

L_____ (Monday)   V_____ (Friday)

M_____ (Tuesday)   S_____ (Saturday)

M_____ (Wednesday)

14. Les Mois / The Months

Find the names of the twelve months of the year. The words may appear vertically, horizontally or diagonally and may overlap or be reversed. Find and circle the hidden words, then write them in the spaces at the bottom of the page (accents, hyphens and ligatures are omitted from the grids). Each word's first letter and English equivalent are provided as clues.

J	S	E	P	T	E	M	B	R	E
U	N	R	A	R	U	T	H	J	R
I	M	B	A	E	L	O	U	A	B
L	A	O	L	I	I	I	A	N	M
L	R	T	I	R	N	E	I	V	E
E	S	C	R	V	M	A	A	I	C
T	N	O	V	E	M	B	R	E	E
M	A	N	A	F	M	E	M	R	D

J_____ (January) J_____ (July)

F_____ (February) A_____ (August)

M_____ (March) S_____ (September)

A_____ (April) O_____ (October)

M_____ (May) N_____ (November)

J_____ (June) D_____ (December)

15. Les Adjectifs II / Adjectives II

Find 20 common adjectives (all are masculine singular forms). The words may appear vertically, horizontally or diagonally and may overlap or be reversed. Find and circle the hidden words, then write them in the spaces at the bottom of the page (accents, hyphens and ligatures are omitted from the grids). Each word's first letter and English equivalent are provided as clues.

M	I	N	C	E	P	X	Z	D	L
A	O	R	E	O	M	E	U	R	A
U	R	U	D	U	U	G	T	O	I
V	I	E	U	X	F	R	O	I	D
A	U	A	E	B	O	O	T	T	T
I	L	O	J	O	R	S	F	I	N
S	A	L	E	N	T	L	O	N	G

b_____ (beautiful)   j_____ (pretty, nice)

b_____ (good)   l_____ (ugly, vile)

c_____ (short)   l_____ (long)

d_____ (soft, sweet)   m_____ (bad)

d_____ (straight)   m_____ (thin)

d_____ (hard, harsh)   m_____ (soft)

f_____ (fine, thin)   n_____ (new)

f_____ (strong, big)   p_____ (small)

f_____ (cold)   s_____ (dirty)

g_____ (big, fat)   v_____ (old)

16. Les Couleurs / Colors

Find the names of nine colors. The words may appear vertically, horizontally or diagonally and may overlap or be reversed. Find and circle the hidden words, then write them in the spaces at the bottom of the page (accents, hyphens and ligatures are omitted from the grids). Each word's first letter and English equivalent are provided as clues.

```
Z   O   B   L   E   U   V

E   B   R   O   U   G   E

E   N   U   A   J   R   R

E   S   N   I   N   I   T

E   S   O   R   O   G   N

B   L   A   N   C   G   E
```

b_____ (white)   o_____ (orange)

b_____ (blue)   r_____ (pink)

b_____ (brown)   r_____ (red)

j_____ (yellow)   v_____ (green)

n_____ (black)

17. Les Animaux Sauvages / Wild Animals

Find the names of twelve wild animals. The words may appear vertically, horizontally or diagonally and may overlap or be reversed. Find and circle the hidden words, then write them in the spaces at the bottom of the page (accents, hyphens and ligatures are omitted from the grids). Each word's first letter and English equivalent are provided as clues.

C	A	S	T	O	R	N	C	A	R	R
H	I	P	P	O	P	O	T	A	M	E
A	N	A	U	V	S	I	N	G	E	N
M	A	R	L	H	G	L	O	U	P	A
E	S	G	I	R	A	F	E	I	V	R
A	E	L	E	O	P	A	R	D	R	D
U	S	W	T	N	A	H	P	E	L	E

c_____ (beaver)   l_____ (lion)

c_____ (camel)   l_____ (wolf)

e_____ (elephant)   o_____ (bear)

g_____ (giraffe)   r_____ (fox)

h_____ (hippopotamus)   s_____ (monkey)

l_____ (leopard)   t_____ (tiger)

18. L'Univers / The Universe

Find nine words pertaining to astronomy. The words may appear vertically, horizontally or diagonally and may overlap or be reversed. Find and circle the hidden words, then write them in the spaces at the bottom of the page (accents, hyphens and ligatures are omitted from the grids). Each word's first letter and English equivalent are provided as clues.

P	C	L	U	N	E	A	S
E	L	I	E	L	O	S	A
B	T	A	E	C	D	E	T
F	G	E	N	L	H	I	U
S	R	A	M	E	J	K	R
L	E	L	I	O	T	E	N
E	R	R	E	T	C	E	E

c_____ (sky)   p_____ (planet)

c_____ (comet)   S_____ (Saturn)

e_____ (star)   s_____ (sun)

l_____ (moon)   T_____ (Earth)

M_____ (Mars)

19. La Classe / The Classroom

Find eleven words relating to a classroom. The words may appear vertically, horizontally or diagonally and may overlap or be reversed. Find and circle the hidden words, then write them in the spaces at the bottom of the page (accents, hyphens and ligatures are omitted from the grids). Each word's first letter and English equivalent are provided as clues.

P	R	O	F	E	S	S	E	U	R
U	E	N	A	L	N	B	F	E	E
P	I	U	C	E	O	H	F	S	G
I	H	O	D	V	Y	O	A	I	L
T	A	B	L	E	A	U	C	A	E
R	C	L	I	V	R	E	E	H	N
E	I	A	R	C	C	A	U	C	S

c_____ (notebook)   l_____ (book)

c_____ (chair)   p_____ (teacher)

c_____ (chalk)   p_____ (desk)

c_____ (pencil)   r_____ (ruler)

e_____ (eraser)   t_____ (blackboard)

e_____ (pupil)

20. Les Sports / Sports

Find the names of 13 sports. The words may appear vertically, horizontally or diagonally and may overlap or be reversed. Find and circle the hidden words, then write them in the spaces at the bottom of the page (accents, hyphens and ligatures are omitted from the grids). Each word's first letter and English equivalent are provided as clues.

B	N	A	T	A	T	I	O	N	T
A	T	H	L	E	T	I	S	M	E
S	A	L	E	K	A	Y	A	K	N
E	S	C	A	L	A	D	E	A	N
B	K	L	A	G	I	E	L	R	I
A	I	U	I	N	O	O	A	A	S
L	A	J	U	D	O	L	V	T	M
L	U	T	T	E	O	T	F	E	E

a_____ (athletics) k_____ (kayaking)

b_____ (baseball) l_____ (wrestling)

c_____ (boating) n_____ (swimming)

e_____ (climbing) s_____ (skiing)

g_____ (golf) t_____ (tennis)

j_____ (judo) v_____ (sailing)

k_____ (karate)

21. Le Paysage / Landscape

Find eleven words relating to a landscape. The words may appear vertically, horizontally or diagonally and may overlap or be reversed. Find and circle the hidden words, then write them in the spaces at the bottom of the page (accents, hyphens and ligatures are omitted from the grids). Each word's first letter and English equivalent are provided as clues.

E	R	E	I	V	I	R
N	C	H	P	R	E	U
G	O	E	U	R	A	E
A	C	L	B	C	A	L
T	E	R	O	F	P	F
N	A	O	I	M	M	R
O	N	E	S	B	E	O
M	C	H	A	M	P	S

a_____ (tree)   m_____ (sea)

b_____ (wood)   m_____ (mountain)

c_____ (fields)   o_____ (ocean)

f_____ (flower)   p_____ (meadow)

f_____ (forest)   r_____ (stream)

l_____ (lake)

22. **La Musique** / Music

Find twelve terms relating to music. The words may appear vertically, horizontally or diagonally and may overlap or be reversed. Find and circle the hidden words, then write them in the spaces at the bottom of the page (accents, hyphens and ligatures are omitted from the grids). Each word's first letter and English equivalent are provided as clues.

P	I	A	N	O	T	H	A
H	M	G	O	F	R	A	R
F	L	U	T	E	O	R	P
V	E	I	E	B	M	M	E
I	S	T	G	A	P	O	G
O	E	A	T	S	E	N	E
L	I	R	V	S	T	I	C
O	D	E	W	E	T	E	L
N	O	R	G	U	E	Z	E

a _____ (arpeggio)

b_____ (bass)

c_____ (clef)

d_____ (sharp)

f_____ (flute)

g_____ (guitar)

h_____ (harmony)

n_____ (note)

o_____ (organ)

p_____ (piano)

t_____ (trumpet)

v_____ (violin)

23. La Religion / Religion

Find ten words relating to religion. The words may appear vertically, horizontally or diagonally and may overlap or be reversed. Find and circle the hidden words, then write them in the spaces at the bottom of the page (accents, hyphens and ligatures are omitted from the grids). Each word's first letter and English equivalent are provided as clues.

D	I	L	E	F	O	I	T	A
I	I	T	U	P	N	E	E	F
E	S	P	E	R	A	N	C	E
U	O	I	S	I	M	O	I	G
B	I	B	L	E	I	E	F	L
O	S	A	C	R	E	T	F	I
C	U	L	T	E	T	U	O	S
I	P	I	P	R	E	T	R	E

B_____ (Bible)   f_____ (faith)

c_____ (worship)   o_____ (service)

D_____ (God)   p_____ (priest)

e_____ (church)   p_____ (prayer)

e_____ (hope)   s_____ (sacred)

24. Les Voitures / Automobiles

Find ten words relating to automobiles. The words may appear vertically, horizontally or diagonally and may overlap or be reversed. Find and circle the hidden words, then write them in the spaces at the bottom of the page (accents, hyphens and ligatures are omitted from the grids). Each word's first letter and English equivalent are provided as clues.

E	M	O	T	E	U	R	P
S	V	Y	U	A	M	F	H
S	A	O	T	E	U	R	A
E	R	C	L	E	F	E	R
N	O	T	O	A	C	I	E
C	A	P	O	T	N	N	A
E	G	E	I	S	S	T	E

c_____ (hood)   p_____ (headlight)

c_____ (key)   r_____ (wheel)

e_____ (gas)   r_____ (street)

f_____ (brake)   s_____ (seat)

m_____ (engine)   v_____ (steering wheel)

CROSSWORDS

25. Les Vêtements / Clothes

Fill in the following crossword puzzle using the French equivalents of the provided English clothing-related words. The first letter of each French word has been filled in as a clue.

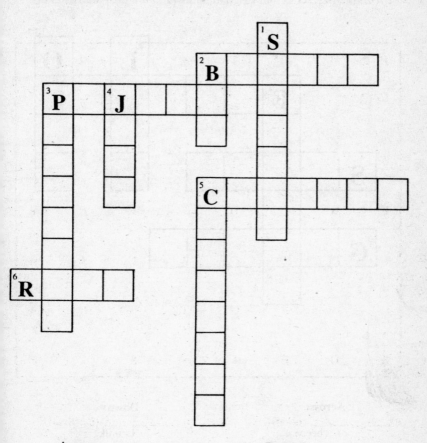

Across:

2. blouse
3. pair of pyjamas
5. shirt
6. dress

Down:

1. shoe
2. stocking
3. pair of trousers
4. skirt
5. sweater

26. Les Comestibles / Foods

Fill in the following crossword puzzle using the French equivalents of the provided English food-related words. The first letter of each French word has been filled in as a clue.

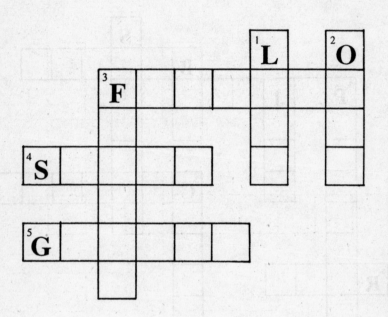

Across:

3. cheese
4. soup
5. cake

Down:

1. milk
2. egg
3. fruit (pl.)

27. Les Vêtements d'Hiver / Winter Clothes

Fill in the following crossword puzzle using the French equivalents of the provided English words relating to winter clothing. The first letter of each French word has been filled in as a clue.

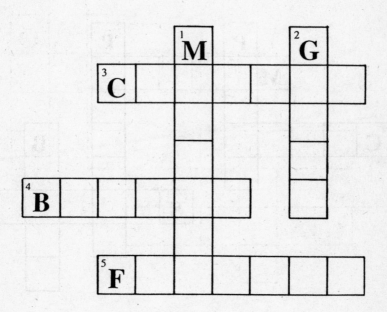

Across:

3. hat
4. boots
5. scarf

Down:

1. coat
2. gloves

28. **Au Restaurant** / At a Restaurant

Fill in the following crossword puzzle using the French infinitive equivalents of the provided English restaurant-related verbs. The first letter of each French verb has been filled in as a clue.

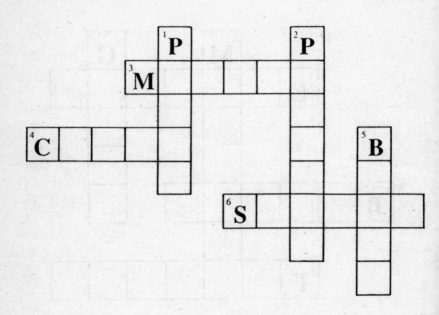

Across:

3. to eat
4. to cook
6. to serve

Down:

1. to pay
2. to take
5. to drink

29. Dans la Cuisine / In the Kitchen

Fill in the following crossword puzzle using the French equivalents of the provided English kitchen-related words. The first letter of each French word has been filled in as a clue.

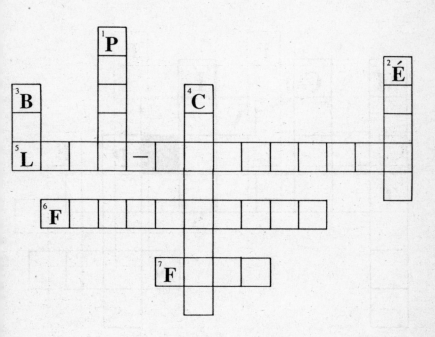

Across:

5. dishwasher
6. refrigerator
7. oven

Down:

1. frying pan
2. sink
3. bowl
4. cauldron

30. Les Outils / Tools

Fill in the following crossword puzzle using the French equivalents of the provided English names for tools. The first letter of each French word has been filled in as a clue.

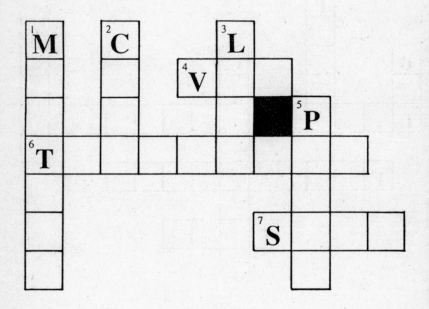

Across:

4. screw
6. screwdriver
7. saw

Down:

1. hammer
2. nail
3. file
5. pliers

31. Les Fleurs / Flowers

Fill in the following crossword puzzle using the French equivalents of the provided English flower names. The first letter of each French word has been filled in as a clue.

Across:

2. lily
5. daisy

Down:

1. violet
3. tulip
4. lilac
5. lily-of-the-valley
6. rose

32. Les Arbres / Trees

Fill in the following crossword puzzle using the French equivalents of the provided English tree names. The first letter of each French word has been filled in as a clue.

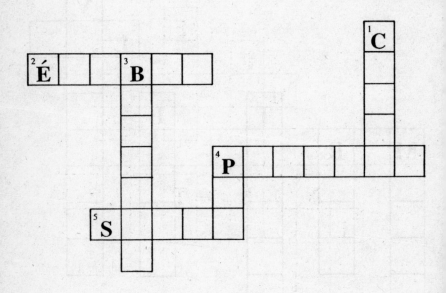

Across:

2. maple
4. palm
5. fir

Down:

1. oak
3. birch
4. pine

33. Les Antonymes / Antonyms

Fill in the following crossword puzzle with the antonyms of the given French words. The first letter of each word in the puzzle has been filled in as a clue, and the English equivalents of the sought-for words are provided.

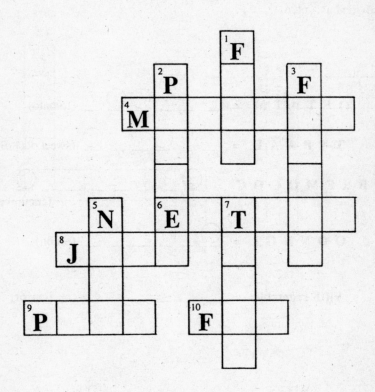

Across:

4. courir : _____ [to walk]
6. sortir : _____ [to enter]
8. nuit : _____ [day]
9. mère : _____ [father]
10. eau : _____ [fire]

Down:

1. dos : _____ [front]
2. écouter : _____ [to talk]
3. ouvrir : _____ [to close]
5. blanc : _____ [black]
7. pousser : _____ [to pull]

JUMBLES

34. Les Légumes / Vegetables

This puzzle contains the French names for four common vegetables in jumbled form. Unscramble the words and write them correctly in the blanks provided, then arrange the letters that fall in circled spaces to form the name of a fifth vegetable. The English equivalent of each word is provided as a clue.

O E T A T M = _ _ _ ⊙ ⊙ _ (tomato)

T T P A A E = _ _ ⊙ _ _ ⊙ (sweet potato)

N B R E M O C O C = ⊙ _ _ _ _ _ _ ⊙ _ (cucumber)

O O N N G I = ⊙ _ _ _ _ _ (onion)

Fifth vegetable = _ _ _ _ _ _ _ (carrot)

35. Les Fruits / Fruits

This puzzle contains the French names for five common fruits in jumbled form (accents have been omitted). Unscramble the words and write them correctly in the blanks provided, then arrange the letters that fall in circled spaces to form the name of a sixth fruit. The English equivalent of each word is provided as a clue.

E M M P O = _ _ _ _ _◯ (apple)

O G R E A N = _ _◯ _ _ _◯ (orange)

N I S I A R = _ _ _ _◯ _ _ (grape)

O I E P R = _ _ _◯ _ _ (pear)

H C E E P = _ _ _◯ _ _ (peach)

Sixth fruit = _ _ _ _ _ _ _ (cherry)

36. Les Quatre Saisons / The Four Seasons

This puzzle contains the French names for the four seasons in jumbled form (accents have been omitted). Unscramble the words and write them correctly in the blanks provided. The English equivalent of each word is provided as a clue.

N P P R S I M E T = _ _ _ _ _ _ _ _ _
(Spring)

T E E = _ _ _ (Summer)

U T M N E O A = _ _ _ _ _ _ _ (Autumn)

V H R E I = _ _ _ _ _ (Winter)

37. Les Créatures de la Mer / Sea Creatures

This puzzle contains the French names of four common sea creatures in jumbled form. Unscramble the words and write them correctly in the blanks provided, then arrange the letters that fall in circled spaces to form the name of a fifth sea creature. The English equivalent of each word is provided as a clue.

U R T I T E = _ _ _ _ _ ⃝ (trout)

U I N Q E R = ⃝ _ _ _ _ _ (shark)

I P A D U H N = _ _ ⃝ _ _ _ _ (dolphin)

S M N A U O = _ _ _ ⃝ ⃝ _ (salmon)

Fifth sea creature = _ _ _ _ _ (cod)

WORD GRIDS

38. Les Métiers / Professions

Write the French equivalents of the given English professions in the numbered spaces provided; after the grid is completed, identify the French word spelled out vertically in the highlighted box and write its English equivalent in the blank provided.

English equivalents:

1. cook
2. butcher
3. baker
4. teacher
5. firefighter
6. physician
7. mechanic
8. artist
9. gardener
10. farmer
11. author

Vertical word: _____

39. Les Caractères / Character Types

Write the French equivalents of the given English character types in the numbered spaces provided; after the grid is completed, identify the French word spelled out vertically in the highlighted box and write its English equivalent in the blank provided.

1	T				T	
2		A				A
3			P		L	
4		J				X
5	B			E		
6	S				X	
7	J		Y			
8	H				T	
9			T			D

English equivalents:

1. sad
2. friendly
3. polite
4. jealous
5. silly

6. serious
7. joyful
8. honest
9. shy

Vertical word: _____

40. Dans la Chambre à Coucher / In the Bedroom

Write the French equivalents of the given English words for objects found in a bedroom in the numbered spaces provided; after the grid is completed, identify the French word spelled out vertically in the highlighted box and write its English equivalent in the blank provided.

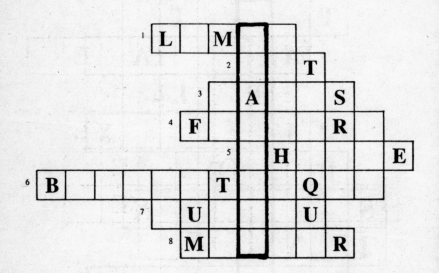

English equivalents:

1. lamp
2. bed
3. carpet
4. window

5. chair
6. bookcase
7. desk
8. mirror

Vertical word: _____

41. À la Bibliothèque / At the Library

Write the French equivalents of the given English library-related terms in the numbered spaces provided; after the grid is completed, identify the French word spelled out vertically in the highlighted box and write its English equivalent in the blank provided.

1	É				È		E	
	2	S			E			
		3	T				E	
	4		E			E		
5	E					E		
6		V		E				

English equivalents:

1. shelves
2. subject
3. title

4. magazines
5. to borrow
6. books

Vertical word: _____

42. La Poste / The Mail

Write the French equivalents of the given English mail-related words in the numbered spaces provided; after the grid is completed, identify the French word spelled out vertically in the highlighted box and write its English equivalent in the blank provided.

		1						
1 E			E				E	
2		O		E				
3				I				E
4			C		E			
5 C						E		
6		D		E		E		

English equivalents:

1. envelopes
2. postal code
3. stamp

4. mail carrier
5. mail
6. address

Vertical word: _____

43. La Ville / The City

Write the French equivalents of the given English city-related words in the numbered spaces provided; after the grid is completed, identify the French word spelled out vertically in the highlighted box and write its English equivalent in the space provided.

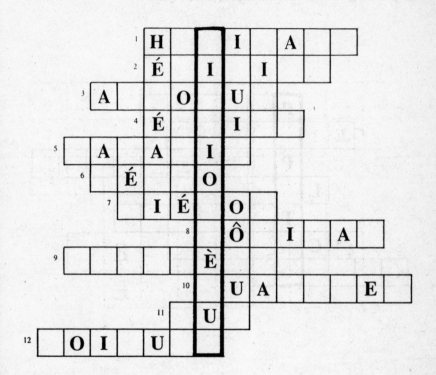

English equivalents:

1. occupant
2. building
3. bus
4. church
5. store
6. subway
7. pedestrian
8. hospital
9. fence
10. district
11. street
12. automobile

Vertical word: _____

44. À la Classe / In the Classroom

Write the French equivalents of the given English classroom-related words in the numbered spaces provided; after the grid is completed, identify the French word spelled out vertically in the highlighted box and write its English equivalent in the space provided.

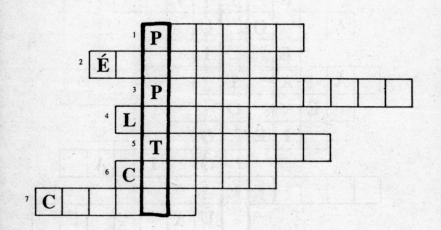

English equivalents:

1. paper
2. square
3. teacher
4. book

5. blackboard
6. pencil
7. notebook

Vertical word: _____

45. L'Aviation / Aviation

Write the French equivalents of the given English aviation-related words in the numbered spaces provided; after the grid is completed, identify the French word spelled out vertically in the highlighted box and write its English equivalent in the space provided.

```
         1  A  □  □  □  □
      2  H  □  □  □  □  □
   3  P  □  □  □  □  □
4  P  □  □  □  □  □
         5  P  □  □  □  □
      6  R  □  □  □  □
   7  P  □  □  □  □
8  B  □  □  □  □  □
```

English equivalents:

1. airplane
2. propellers
3. porter
4. pilot

5. runway
6. wheel
7. gate
8. ticket

Vertical word: _____

SOLUTIONS
Search-a-Words

1. La Famille / The Family

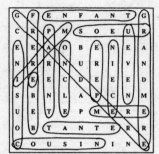

b **ébé** (baby)
c **ousin** (cousin [M])
c **ousine** (cousin [F])
e **nfant** (child)
f **rère** (brother)
g **rand-mère** (grandmother)
g **rand-père** (grandfather)
m **ari** (husband)

m **ère** (mother)
n **eveu** (nephew)
n **ièce** (niece)
o **ncle** (uncle)
p **arent** (relative)
p **ère** (father)
s **oeur** (sister)
t **ante** (aunt)

2. Le Corps / The Body

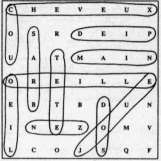

b **ras** (arm)
c **heveux** (hair)
c **ou** (neck)
d **os** (back)
j **oue** (cheek)
m **ain** (hand)

n **ez** (nose)
œil (eye)
o **reille** (ear)
p **ied** (foot)
t **ête** (head)

3. Les Adjectifs I / Adjectives I

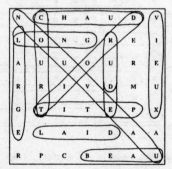

b **eau** (beautiful)
c **haud** (warm; hot)
c **ourt** (short)
d **roit** (straight)
d **ur** (hard)
l **aid** (ugly)

l **arge** (wide; broad)
l **ong** (long)
n **ouveau** (new)
p **etit** (small; young)
r **ude** (rough)
v **ieux** (old)

4. La Maison / The House

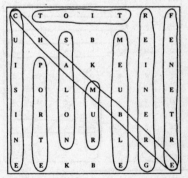

c **hambre** ([bed]room)
c **uisine** (kitchen)
f **enêtre** (window)
g **renier** (attic, loft)
m **euble** (piece of furniture)

m **ur** (wall)
p **orte** (door)
s **alon** (living room)
t **oit** (roof)

5. Le Temps / Weather

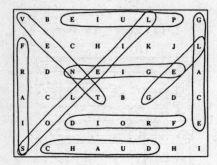

e **haud** (hot)
r **rais** (cool)
r **roid** (cold)
g **el** (frost)
g **lace** (ice)

n **eige** (snow)
p **luie** (rain)
s **oleil** (sun)
v **ent** (wind)

6. Les Animaux de Basse-cour / Farm Animals

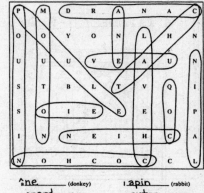

â **ne** (donkey)
c **anard** (duck)
c **hat** (cat [M])
c **heval** (horse)
c **hien** (dog [M])
c **ochon** (pig)
c **oq** (rooster)

l **apin** (rabbit)
m **outon** (sheep)
o **ie** (goose)
p **oule** (hen)
p **oussin** (chick)
v **eau** (calf)

7. Le Transport / Transportation

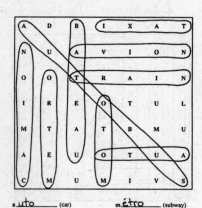

a **uto** (car)
a **utobus** (bus)
a **vion** (airplane)
b **ateau** (boat)
c **amion** (truck)

m **étro** (subway)
m **oto** (motorcycle)
t **axi** (taxicab)
t **rain** (train)

8. Au Téléphone / On the Telephone

M	A	S	P	A	R	L	E	R	A
T	E	L	E	P	H	O	N	E	R
M	C	O	M	P	O	S	E	R	S
A	E	M	R	E	T	U	O	C	E
S	R	R	E	L	E	P	P	A	R
A	I	M	R	E	N	N	O	S	M
S	D	E	C	R	O	C	H	E	R

a **ppeler** (to call)
c **omposer** (to dial)
d **écrocher** (to pick up [the receiver])
d **ire** (to say)
é **couter** (to listen)

p **arler** (to talk)
r **appeler** (to call back)
s **onner** (to ring)
t **éléphoner** (to phone)

9. Les Salutations / Greetings

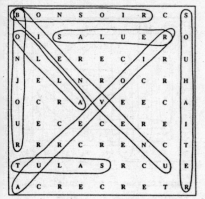

a llô _____ (hello [on phone])

a ll revoir _____ (so long)

b ienvenu _____ (welcome)

b onjour _____ (good morning)

b onsoir _____ (good evening)

s aluer _____ (to greet)

s alut _____ (hi)

s ouhaiter _____ (to wish)

10. Le Voyage / Travel

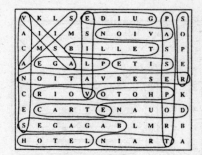

a mis _____ (friends [M])

a vion _____ (airplane)

b agages _____ (luggage)

b illet _____ (ticket)

c arte _____ (map)

d ouane _____ (customs)

g uide _____ (guide)

h ôtel _____ (hotel)

p asseport _____ (passport)

p hoto _____ (photograph)

p lage _____ (beach)

r epos _____ (rest)

r éservation _____ (reservation)

s ite _____ (point of interest)

t rain _____ (train)

v acances _____ (vacation)

v alise _____ (suitcase)

v isa _____ (visa)

v oir _____ (to see)

11. Au Bord de la Mer / At the Beach

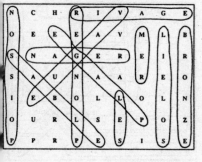

b ronzé _____ (tanned)

m er _____ (sea)

n ager _____ (to swim)

p lage _____ (beach)

p longer _____ (to dive)

p oisson _____ (fish)

r ivage _____ (shore)

s able _____ (sand)

s el _____ (salt)

s oleil _____ (sun)

v ague _____ (wave)

12. Les Pays / Countries

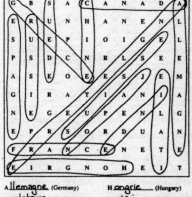

A llemagne _____ (Germany)

A ngleterre _____ (England)

c anada _____ (Canada)

c hine _____ (China)

E spagne _____ (Spain)

F rance _____ (France)

G rèce _____ (Greece)

H ongrie _____ (Hungary)

I nde _____ (India)

I talie _____ (Italy)

J apon _____ (Japan)

R ussie _____ (Russia)

s uède _____ (Sweden)

s uisse _____ (Switzerland)

13. Les Jours de la Semaine / The Days of the Week

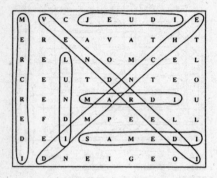

Dimanche (Sunday)
Lundi (Monday)
Mardi (Tuesday)
Mercredi (Wednesday)
Jeudi (Thursday)
Vendredi (Friday)
Samedi (Saturday)

14. Les Mois / The Months

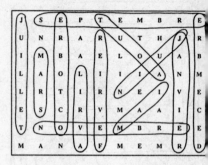

Janvier (January)
Février (February)
Mars (March)
Avril (April)
Mai (May)
Juin (June)
Juillet (July)
Août (August)
Septembre (September)
Octobre (October)
Novembre (November)
Décembre (December)

15. Les Adjectifs II / Adjectives II

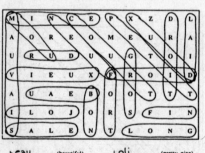

beau (beautiful)
bon (good)
court (short)
doux (soft, sweet)
droit (straight)
dur (hard, harsh)
fin (fine, thin)
fort (strong, big)
froid (cold)
gros (big, fat)
joli (pretty, nice)
laid (ugly, vile)
long (long)
mauvais (bad)
mince (thin)
mou (soft)
neuf (new)
petit (small)
sale (dirty)
vieux (old)

16. Les Couleurs / Colors

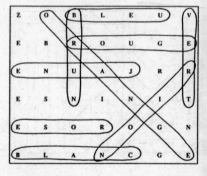

blanc (white)
bleu (blue)
brun (brown)
jaune (yellow)
noir (black)
orange (orange)
rose (pink)
rouge (red)
vert (green)

17. Les Animaux Sauvages / Wild Animals

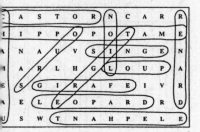

C	A	S	T	O	R	N	C	A	R	R
H	I	P	P	O	P	O	T	A	M	E
A	N	A	U	V	S	I	N	G	E	N
M	A	R	L	H	G	L	O	U	P	A
E	S	G	I	R	A	F	E	I	V	R
A	E	L	E	O	P	A	R	D	R	D
U	S	W	T	N	A	H	P	E	L	E

c**astor** (beaver)
c**ameou** (camel)
él**éphant** (elephant)
gi**rafe** (giraffe)
h**ppopotame** (hippopotamus)
lé**opard** (leopard)

l**ion** (lion)
l**oup** (wolf)
o**urs** (bear)
r**enard** (fox)
s**inge** (monkey)
t**igre** (tiger)

18. L'Univers / The Universe

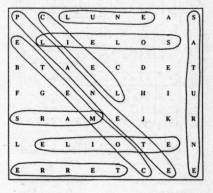

P	C	L	U	N	E	A	S
E	L	I	E	L	O	S	A
B	T	A	E	C	D	E	T
F	G	E	N	L	H	I	U
S	R	A	M	E	J	K	R
L	E	L	I	O	T	E	N
E	R	R	E	T	C	E	E

c**iel** (sky)
c**omète** (comet)
é**toile** (star)
l**une** (moon)
M**ars** (Mars)

p**lanète** (planet)
s**aturne** (Saturn)
s**oleil** (sun)
T**erre** (Earth)

19. La Classe / The Classroom

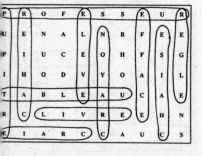

P	R	O	F	E	S	S	E	U	R
U	E	N	A	L	N	B	F	E	E
P	I	U	C	E	O	H	F	S	G
I	H	O	D	V	Y	O	A	I	L
T	A	B	L	E	A	U	C	A	E
R	C	L	I	V	R	E	E	H	N
E	I	A	R	C	C	A	U	C	S

c**ahier** (notebook)
c**haise** (chair)
c**raie** (chalk)
c**rayon** (pencil)
e**fface** (eraser)
é**lève** (pupil)

l**ivre** (book)
p**rofesseur** (teacher)
p**upitre** (desk)
r**ègle** (ruler)
t**ableau** (blackboard)

20. Les Sports / Sports

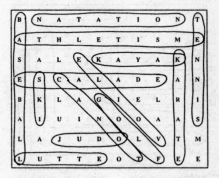

B	N	A	T	A	T	I	O	N	T
A	T	H	L	E	T	I	S	M	E
S	A	L	E	K	A	Y	A	K	N
E	S	C	A	L	A	D	E	A	N
B	K	L	A	G	I	E	L	R	I
A	I	U	I	N	O	O	A	S	S
L	A	J	U	D	O	L	V	T	M
L	U	T	T	E	O	T	F	E	E

a**thlétisme** (athletics)
b**ase-ball** (baseball)
c**anot** (boating)
e**scalade** (climbing)
g**olf** (golf)
j**udo** (judo)
k**araté** (karate)

k**ayak** (kayaking)
l**utte** (wrestling)
n**atation** (swimming)
s**ki** (skiing)
t**ennis** (tennis)
v**oile** (sailing)

21. Le Paysage / Landscape

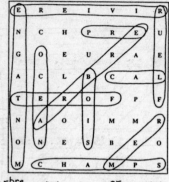

a rbre _____ (tree)
b ois _____ (wood)
c hamps _____ (fields)
f leur _____ (flower)
f orêt _____ (forest)
l ac _____ (lake)

m er _____ (sea)
m ontagne (mountain)
o céan _____ (ocean)
p ré _____ (meadow)
r ivière _____ (stream)

22. La Musique / Music

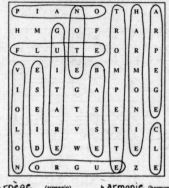

a rpège _____ (arpeggio)
b asse _____ (bass)
c lé _____ (clef)
d ièse _____ (sharp)
f lûte _____ (flute)
g uitare _____ (guitar)

h armonie _____ (harmony)
n ote _____ (note)
o rgue _____ (organ)
p iano _____ (piano)
t rompette _____ (trumpet)
v iolon _____ (violin)

23. La Religion / Religion

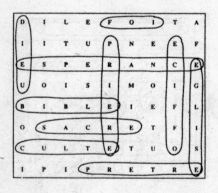

B ible _____ (Bible)
c ulte _____ (worship)
D ieu _____ (God)
é glise _____ (church)
e spérance (hope)

f oi _____ (faith)
o ffice _____ (service)
p rêtre _____ (priest)
p rière _____ (prayer)
s acré _____ (sacred)

24. Les Voitures / Automobiles

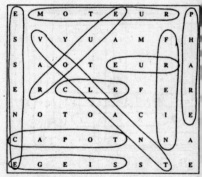

c apot _____ (hood)
c lé _____ (key)
e ssence _____ (gas)
f rein _____ (brake)
m oteur _____ (engine)

p hare _____ (headlight)
r oue _____ (wheel)
r ue _____ (street)
s iège _____ (seat)
v olant _____ (steering wheel)

Crosswords

25. Les Vêtements / Clothes   **26. Les Comestibles** / Foods

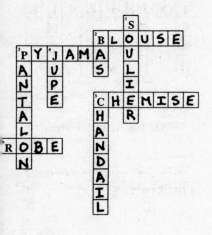 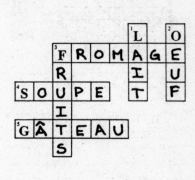

27. Les Vêtements d'Hiver / Winter Clothes   **28. Au Restaurant** / At a Restaurant

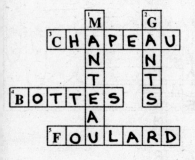 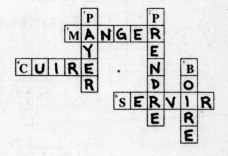

29. Dans la Cuisine / In the Kitchen

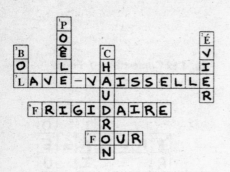

30. Les Outils / Tools

31. Les Fleurs / Flowers

32. Les Arbres / Trees

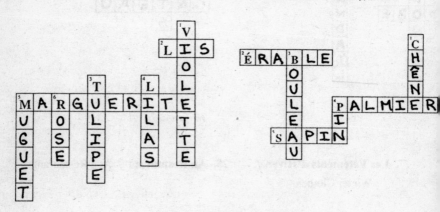

33. Les Antonymes / Antonyms

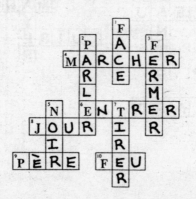

Jumbles

34. Les Légumes / Vegetables

OETATM = t o m a t e (tomato)

TTPAAE = p a t a t e (sweet potato)

NBREMOCOC = c o n c o m b r e (cucumber)

OONNGI = o i g n o n (onion)

Fifth vegetable = c a r o t t e (carrot)

35. Les Fruits / Fruits

EMMPO = p o m m e (apple)

OGREAN = o r a n g e (orange)

NISIAR = r a i s i n (grape)

OIEPR = p o i r e (pear)

HCEEP = p ê c h e (peach)

Sixth fruit = c e r i s e (cherry)

36. Les Quatre Saisons / The Four Seasons

NPPRSIMET = p r i n t e m p s (Spring)

TEE = é t é (Summer)

UTMNEOA = a u t o m n e (Autumn)

VHREI = h i v e r (Winter)

37. Les Créatures de la Mer / Sea Creatures

URTITE = t r u i t e (trout)

UINQER = r e q u i n (shark)

IPADUHN = d a u p h i n (dolphin)

SMNAUO = s a u m o n (salmon)

Fifth sea creature = m o r u e (cod)

Word Grids

38. Les Métiers / Professions

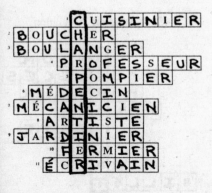

Vertical word: carpenter

39. Les Caractères / Character Types

Vertical word: impatient

40. Dans la Chambre à Coucher / In the Bedroom

Vertical word: floor

41. À la Bibliothèque / At the Library

Vertical word: author

42. La Poste / The Mail

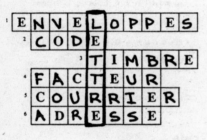

Vertical word: letter

43. La Ville / The City

Vertical word: library

44. À la Classe / In the Classroom

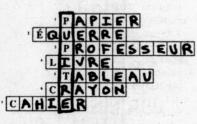

Vertical word: desk

45. L'Aviation / Aviation

Vertical word: airport

ALPHABETICAL WORD LIST

(In the list below, *le* is the article used for masculine singular nouns, *la* for feminine singular. In the cases of plural nouns (for which the article is always *les*) and of nouns beginning with a vowel or silent *h* (article always *l'*), the gender is indicated immediately after the article by the abbreviations M for masculine and F for feminine.)

adjectif, l' (M): adjective
adresse, l' (F): address
aéroport, l' (M): airport
Allemagne, l' (F): Germany
allô: hello
ami, l' (M): friend (M)
amical: friendly
âne, l' (M): donkey
Angleterre, l' (F): England
animal, l' (M): animal
antonyme, l' (M): antonym
août, l' (M): August
appeler: to call
arbre, l' (M): tree
arpège, l' (M): arpeggio
artiste, l' (M): artist
athlétisme, l' (M): athletics
au revoir: so long
auteur, l' (M): author
auto, l' (F): car
autobus, l' (M): bus
automne, l' (M): autumn
aviation, l' (F): aviation
avion, l' (M): airplane
avril, l' (M): April

bagages, les (M): luggage
barrière, la: fence
bas, le: stocking
base-ball, le: baseball
basse, la: bass
basse-cour, la: farmyard
bateau, le: boat
beau: beautiful
bébé, le: baby
bête: silly
Bible, la: Bible
bibliothèque, la: library, bookcase
bienvenu: welcome
billet, le: ticket
blanc: white

bleu: blue
blouse, la: blouse
boire: to drink
bois, le: wood
bol, le: bowl
bon: good
bonjour: good morning
bonsoir: good evening
bord, le: edge
bottes, les (F): boots
boucher, le: butcher
boulanger, le: baker
bouleau, le: birch
bras, le: arm
bronzé: suntanned
brun: brown
bureau, le: desk

cahier, le: notebook
camion, le: truck
Canada, le: Canada
canard, le: duck
canot, le: boating
capot, le: hood
caractère, le: character
carotte, la: carrot
carte, la: map
castor, le: beaver
cerise, la: cherry
chaise, la: chair
chambre, la: [bed]room
chameau, le: camel
champ, le: field
chandail, le: sweater
chapeau, le: hat
charpentier, le: carpenter
chat, le: cat (M)
chaud: warm, hot
chaudron, le: cauldron
chemise, la: shirt
chêne, le: oak

cheval, le: horse
cheveu, le: hair
chien, le: dog (M)
Chine, la: China
ciel, le: sky
classe, la: classroom
clé, la: clef
clou, le: nail
cochon, le: pig
code, le: postal code
comestibles, les (M): foods
comète, la: comet
composer: to dial
concombre, le: cucumber
coq, le: rooster
corps, le: body
cou, le: neck
coucher: to go to bed
couleur, la: color
courir: to run
courrier, le: mail
court: short
cousin, le: cousin (M)
cousine, la: cousin (F)
craie, la: chalk
crayon, le: pencil
créature, la: creature
cuire: to cook
cuisine, la: kitchen
cuisinier, le: cook
culte, le: worship

dauphin, le: dolphin
décembre, le: December
décrocher: to pick up (the telephone receiver)
dièse, le: sharp
Dieu, le: God
dimanche, le: Sunday
dire: to say
dos, le: back
douane, la: customs
doux: soft, sweet
droit: straight
dur: hard, harsh

eau, l' (F): water
écouter: to listen
écrivain, l' (M): author
édifice, l' (M): building

efface, l' (F): eraser
église, l' (F): church
éléphant, l' (M): elephant
élève, l' (M/F): pupil
emprunter: to borrow
enfant, l' (M/F): child
entrer: to enter
enveloppe, l' (F): envelope
équerre, l' (F): square
érable, l' (M): maple
escalade, l' (F): climbing
Espagne, l' (F): Spain
espérance, l' (F): hope
essence, l' (F): gasoline
étagère, l' (F): shelf
été, l' (M): summer
étoile, l' (F): star
évier, l' (M): sink

face, la: front
facteur, le: mail carrier
famille, la: family
fenêtre, la: window
fermer: to close
fermier, le: farmer
feu, le: fire
février, le: February
fin: fine, thin
fleur, la: flower
flûte, la: flute
foi, la: faith
forêt, la: forest
fort: strong, big
foulard, le: scarf
four, le: oven
frais: cool
France, la: France
frein, le: brake
frère, le: brother
frigidaire, le: refrigerator
froid: cold
fromage, le: cheese
fruit, le: fruit

gants, les (M): gloves
gâteau, le: cake
gel, le: frost
girafe, la: giraffe
glace, la: ice
golf, le: golf

grand-mère, la: grandmother
grand-père, le: grandfather
Grèce, la: Greece
grenier, le: attic; loft
gros: big, fat
guide, le: guide
guitare, la: guitar

habitant, l' (M): occupant
harmonie, l' (F): harmony
hélice, l' (F): propeller
hippopotame, l' (M): hippopotamus
hiver, l' (M): winter
Hongrie, l' (F): Hungary
honnête: honest
hôpital, l' (M): hospital
hôtel, l' (M): hotel

impatient: impatient
Inde, l' (F): India
Italie, l' (F): Italy

jaloux: jealous
janvier, le: January
Japon, le: Japan
jardinier, le: gardener
jaune: yellow
jeudi, le: Thursday
joli: pretty, nice
joue, la: cheek
jour, le: day
joyeux: joyful
judo, le: judo
juillet, le: July
juin, le: June
jupe, la: skirt

karaté, le: karate
kayak, le: kayaking

lac, le: lake
laid: ugly, vile
lait, le: milk
lampe, la: lamp
lapin, le: rabbit
large: wide, broad
lave-vaisselle, le: dishwasher
légume, le: vegetable
léopard, le: leopard
lettre, la: letter

lilas, le: lilac
lime, la: file
lion, le: lion
lis, le: lily
lit, le: bed
livre, le: book
long: long
loup, le: wolf
lundi, le: Monday
lune, la: moon
lutte, la: wrestling

magasin, le: store
mai, le: May
main, la: hand
maison, la: house
manger: to eat
manteau, le: coat
marchèr: to walk
mardi, le: Tuesday
marguerite, la: daisy
mari, le: husband
mars, le: March, Mars
marteau, le: hammer
mauvais: bad
mécanicien, le: mechanic
médecin, le: physician
mer, la: sea
mercredi, le: Wednesday
mère, la: mother
métier, le: profession
métro, le: subway
meuble, le: piece of furniture
mince: thin
miroir, le: mirror
mois, le: month
montagne, la: mountain
morue, la: cod
moteur, le: engine
moto, la: motorcycle
mou: soft
mouton, le: sheep
muguet, le: lily-of-the-valley
mur, le: wall
musique, la: music

nager: to swim
natation, la: swiming
neige, la: snow
neuf: new

neveu, le: nephew
nez, le: nose
nièce, la: niece
noir: black
note, la: note
nouveau: new
novembre, le: November
nuit, la: night

océan, l' (M): ocean
octobre, l' (M): October
œil, l' (M): eye
œuf, l' (M): egg
office, l' (M): service
oie, l' (F): goose
oignon, l' (M): onion
oncle, l' (M): uncle
orange: orange (color)
orange, l' (F): orange
oreille, l' (F): ear
orgue, l' (M): organ
ours, l' (M): bear
outil, l' (M): tool
ouvrir: to open

palmier, le: palm tree
pantalon, le: pair of trousers
papier, le: paper
parent, le: relative
parler: to talk
passeport, le: passport
patate, la: sweet potato
payer: to pay
pays, le: country
paysage, le: landscape
pêche, la: peach
père, le: father
petit: small, young
phare, le: headlight
photo, la: photograph
piano, le: piano
pied, le: foot
piéton, le: pedestrian
pilote, le: pilot
pin, le: pine
pince, la: pliers
piste, la: runway
plage, la: beach
plancher, le: floor
planète, la: planet

plonger: to dive
pluie, la: rain
poêle, la: frying pan
poire, la: pear
poisson, le: fish
poli: polite
pomme, la: apple
pompier, le: firefighter
porte, la: door, gate
porteur, le: porter
poste, la: mail
poule, la: hen
pousser: to push
poussin, le: chick
pré, le: meadow
prendre: to take
prêtre, le: priest
prière, la: prayer
printemps, le: spring
professeur, le: teacher
pupitre, le: desk
pyjama, le: pair of pyjamas

quartier, le: district
quatre: four

raisin, le: grape
rappeler: to call back
règle, la: ruler
religion, la: religion
renard, le: fox
repos, le: rest
requin, le: shark
réservation, la: reservation
restaurant, le: restaurant
revue, la: magazine
rivage, le: shore
rivière, la: stream
robe, la: dress
rose: pink
rose, la: rose
roue, la: wheel
rouge: red
rude: rough
rue, la: street
Russie, la: Russia

sable, le: sand
sacré: sacred
saison, la: season

sale: dirty
salon, le: lounge
saluer: to greet
salut: hi
salutation, la: greeting
samedi, le: Saturday
sapin, le: fir
Saturne, le: Saturn
saumon, le: salmon
sauvage: wild
scie, la: saw
sel, le: salt
semaine, la: week
septembre, le: September
sérieux: serious
servir: to serve
siège, le: seat
singe, le: monkey
site, le: point of interest
ski, le: skiing
sœur, la: sister
soleil, le: sun
sonner: to ring
sortir: to exit
souhaiter: to wish
soulier, le: shoe
soupe, la: soup
sport, le: sport
Suède, la: Sweden
Suisse, la: Switzerland
sujet, le: subject

tableau, le: blackboard
tante, la: aunt
tapis, le: carpet
taxi, le: taxicab
téléphone, le: telephone
téléphoner: to phone
temps, le: weather

tennis, le: tennis
Terre, la: Earth
tête, la: head
tigre, le: tiger
timbre, le: stamp
timide: shy
tirer: to pull
titre, le: title
toit, le: roof
tomate, la: tomato
tournevis, le: screwdriver
train, le: train
transport, le: transportation
triste: sad
trompette, la: trumpet
truite, la: trout
tulipe, la: tulip

univers, l' (M): universe

vacances, les (F): vacation
vague, la: wave
valise, la: suitcase
veau, le: calf
vendredi, le: Friday
vent, le: wind
vert: green
vêtement, le: article of clothing
vieux: old
ville, la: city
violette, la: violet
violon, le: violin
vis, la: screw
visa, le: visa
voile, la: sailing
voir: to see
voiture, la: automobile
volant, le: steering wheel
voyage, le: travel

DOVER BOOKS ON LANGUAGE

FIVE GREAT GERMAN SHORT STORIES/ FÜNF DEUTSCHE MEISTERERZÄHLUNGEN: A DUAL-LANGUAGE BOOK, Stanley Appelbaum, (ed.) (Available in United States only). (27619-8) $7.95

INTRODUCTION TO FRENCH POETRY: A DUAL-LANGUAGE BOOK, Stanley Appelbaum (ed.) (26711-3) $3.95

INTERNATIONAL AIRLINE PHRASE BOOK IN SIX LANGUAGES, Joseph W. Bator. (22017-6) $5.95

EGYPTIAN LANGUAGE: EASY LESSONS IN EGYPTIAN HIEROGLYPHICS, Sir E.A. Wallis Budge. (Except United Kingdom). (21394-3) $5.95

INTRODUCTION TO SPANISH POETRY: A DUAL-LANGUAGE BOOK, Eugenio Florit (ed.) (26712-1) $3.95

FRENCH STORIES/ CONTES FRANÇAIS: A DUAL-LANGUAGE BOOK, Wallace Fowlie. (26443-2) $8.95

ANALYTIC DICTIONARY OF CHINESE AND SINO-JAPANESE, Bernhard Karlgren. (26887-X) $12.95

INTRODUCTION TO GERMAN POETRY: A DUAL-LANGUAGE BOOK, Gustave Mathieu and Guy Stern (eds.) (26713-X) $3.95

MODERN CHINESE: A BASIC COURSE (BOOK ONLY), Faculty of Peking University. (22755-3) $4.95

MODERN CHINESE: A BASIC COURSE (CASSETTE EDITION), Faculty of Peking University. (99910-6) 3 cassettes, manual $15.95

INTRODUCTION TO ITALIAN POETRY: A DUAL-LANGUAGE BOOK, Luciano Rebay (ed.) (26715-6) $3.95

CONVERSATIONAL CHINESE FOR BEGINNERS, Morris Swadesh. (21123-1) $3.95

ELEMENTARY TURKISH, Lewis Thomas. (25064-4) $6.95

A MAYA GRAMMAR, Alfred M. Tozzer. (23465-7) $6.95

CANDIDE: A DUAL-LANGUAGE BOOK, Voltaire. (27625-2) $7.95

AN ETYMOLOGICAL DICTIONARY OF MODERN ENGLISH, Ernest Weekley. (21873-2, 21874-0) $21.90

AN INTRODUCTION TO PORTUGUESE GRAMMAR, Edwin B. Williams. (23278-6) $5.95

FLOWERS OF EVIL/FLEURS DU MAL, Charles Baudelaire. (27092-0) $8.95

LATIN SELECTIONS/FLORILEGIUM LATINUM, Moses Hadas and Thomas Suits. (27059-9) $8.95

MODERN FRENCH POETS, Wallace Fowlie (ed.) (27323-7) $7.95

FIRST SPANISH READER, Angel Flores (ed.). (25810-6) $5.95

ITALIAN STORIES/NOVELLE ITALIANE: A DUAL-LANGUAGE BOOK, Robert A. Hall, Jr. (ed.) (26180-8) $7.95

RUSSIAN STORIES/РУССКИЕ РассКазы: A DUAL-LANGUAGE BOOK, Gleb Struve (ed.). (26244-8) $8.95

SPANISH STORIES/CUENTOS ESPAÑOLES: A DUAL-LANGUAGE BOOK, Angel Flores (ed.). (25399-6) $7.95